Youth Arise! A Poetic Call to Empowerment

Copyright © 2010 by Ella Coleman
All rights reserved. No part of this publication may be reproduced, distributed, or transmitted in any form or by any means, including photocopying, recording, or other electronic or mechanical methods, without the prior written permission of the publisher, except in the case of brief quotations embodied in critical reviews and certain other noncommercial uses permitted by copyright law.

EllaVation Publishing, LLC
P.O. Box 361895
Columbus, Ohio 43236

www.EllaVationPublishing.com
books@ellavationpublishing.com

Ordering information:
Special discounts are available on quantity purchases by churches, businesses, organizations, and others. For details, contact the publisher at the address above.

ISBN 978-0-9848025-5-5

First Printing, 2011
Printed in the United States of America

Dedication & Acknowledgements

This book of poetry is dedicated to the youth in my family, church, community, and all over the world. To parents, grandparents, guardians, teachers, pastors, aunts, uncles, mentors and others who contribute to the lives of young people.

I especially thank God, who makes all things possible in my life, including this book. I thank my mother, Era, for her faithful support. I thank my students and other young people who heard or read this poetry and offered helpful feedback. Blessings and gratitude to Senior Pastors Eric and Carolyn Warren of Equip U Ministries for their prayers and spiritual guidance in my life. Special thanks to André Hawkins for his creative input and support. Also, my gratitude goes to Melanie Houston and Monica Warren, for their editorial prowess in perfecting this work.

Table of Contents

4	Introduction	39	Opt Out of Violence
6	Uniquely You	40	The Power Choice
8	What You Say	42	The Deceptive Duo
9	Receive, Give & Sow	44	Look at You…You're Beautiful!
10	The Prince Appeal: A Young Man Alert	46	Seasons' Greetings
		51	Dancing Over the Ocean…Kite Flight
12	Royalty Restoration… The Princess Call	52	Watch, Listen or Eject
		53	Good Thoughts Pursue
14	Respectfully Yours	54	Trans-Parent
15	Dog B-Gone-It!	57	Forgiveness Begin
16	Be Real	58	Youth Empowerment Affirmations
17	Come Clean!	60	Hotlines to Help Directory
18	Jeans Too Tight With Me		60 Bullying
20	Meet Me @ The Mall		Child Abuse
21	Cell Phone Chat…Possibilities		61 Dating Abuse
22	Just a Text Send		Domestic Violence
23	Rejecting 'Sexting'		Drug & Alcohol Abuse
24	Socialite Craze in Cyberspace		62 Depression & Suicide
26	The Credit Trap		Gang Violence
28	Conspiracy Revealed		Health Issues
31	School/Be Not Drug Along		63 Homelessness
32	What-Ever		Human Trafficking
34	One With Your Dream		Pregnancy Help/Support
36	Saint Teen		64 Runaways
37	Pew Pressure		General Help & Opportunities
38	No Bullying		

Introduction

Creativity, truth and fun converge poetically in this book. The poems address the interests, lifestyles, culture, concerns, problems and potential of young people today. Each poem is accompanied by complimentary photos and artwork to enhance its message. They are designed to make you think, laugh, and make positive changes in your life.

Words are powerful. They can be used to build up and empower or to tear down. What we hear and what we listen to will help us, do nothing for us, or hurt us. An artistic genre for youth to express themselves through spoken words with music and rhythms emerged when rap and hip hop began. The "be seen but not heard" syndrome from previous generations faded out to young urban voices speaking loud and clear. Although some of their words were positive and empowering, many of them were demeaning and disrespectful.

The positive and the negative of rap and hip hop have impacted the world and formed a dominant culture among the younger generations worldwide. Rap and hip hop artists influence the music industry, clothes, fashions, mannerisms, facial expressions, thought and speech patterns; all through the presentation of words, motions, dress code and music.

Poetry used strategically can be just as empowering. As an art form, poetry is ancient and empowered many people thousands of years before rap or hip hop was ever heard of. Certainly, poetry in a modern and unique style can be used by youth to voice messages that will uplift, educate, entertain, and point them in the right direction.

The young generation will lead the way into the future with vision and innovation. In spite of being faced with so much opposition and adversity, youth arise! You deserve better than the world offers. Reach for all God has for you by first seeking Him. The best must come from within you to bring solutions to a distressed society.

These writings are presented to inspire, challenge and empower you. The rhyme, reason and rhythm of the poems are designed to come to life as you read or recite them to yourself, family, friends, peers, and even at public events. Also, you are encouraged to write your own poetry and recite it boldly with power. This is one of the main reasons for writing *Youth Arise! A Poetic Call to Empowerment*. Enjoy.

Ella Coleman

The Poetic Empowerment Zone

Uniquely You

Billions of people
Fill the world
But not one is like you
Boy or girl

No matter how
Populations explode
Once you were formed
God withdrew the mold

Your fingerprints
Are like no other
Mother, father
Sister or brother

Who you really are
Is who I aim to see
Regardless of your label
May this truth set you free

Although you may desire
Fame, fortune or wealth
You'll find nothing comparable
To your true authentic self

The sound of your voice
Gestures and mannerisms, too
Boldly declare
You're uniquely you

What You Say

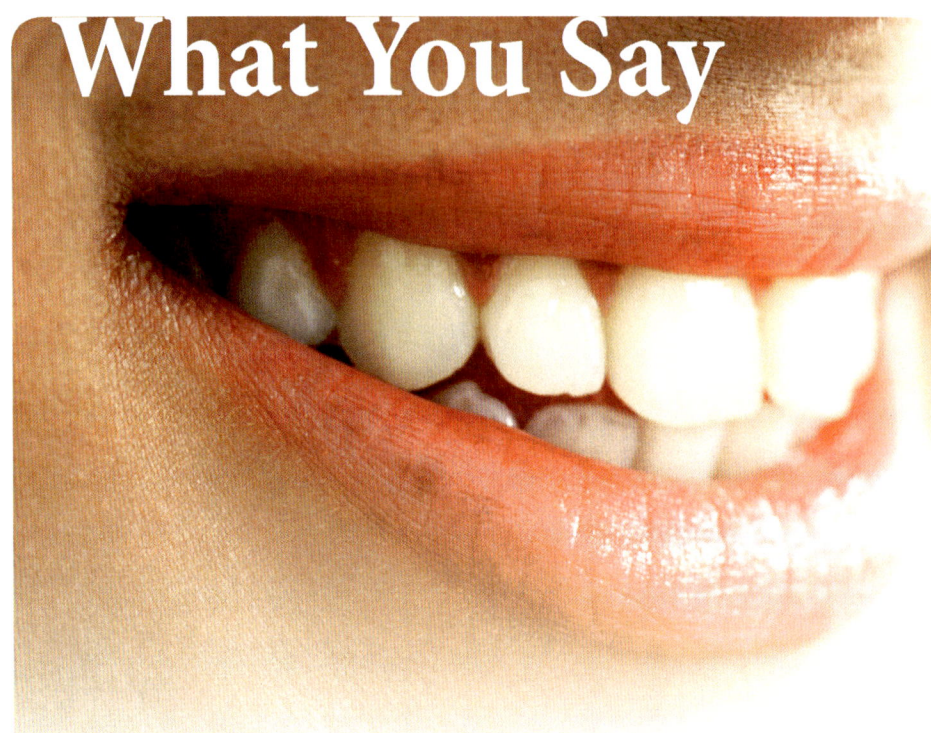

What you say
Loosed by the tongue
Will go its way
To do right or wrong

The words you release
Like magnets attract
Right back to you
Plenty good or lack

Those who speak
Harshly with insults
Reap for themselves
Unfruitful results

Words are powerful
More than you know
They create bondage
Or freedom to go

What's repeatedly voiced
Forms an atmosphere
Conducive to the words
You continuously hear

Determine now
To protect your ears
From destructive messages
That rob youthful years

So remember to think
Before you talk
What you say lingers
Long after you walk

Speaking words of life
In a positive tone
Helps you overcome
'Til negatives are gone

Receive, Give & Sow

Deep within the vault
Of the inner you
Lies rare treasures
Like a brilliant hue
And when taken out
Sparkle brightly new

Oh the gifts that you contain
Unexpressed they'll waste away
Inside they mustn't remain
But be drawn out
So you and others gain

At first you may be nervous
Open up and release all fear
To clear the way for purpose
And prepare the atmosphere
For your gifts to surface

Let creative expression flow
Like lively streams and rivers
On which sunlight shimmers glow
Beaming gifts divinely given
To receive, give and sow

The Prince Appeal:
A Young Man Alert

Summoning young men
From far and near
Precious seed carriers
This message please hear

The strike at your life
Is no coincidence
Your value is priceless
More than can be spent

Pray to receive
The revelation of you
To understand your worth
And your mind renew

You have been called
To royal nobility
But you can only answer
With a heart of sincerity

You bearers of seeds
For future generations
Your family needs you
Alive for duration

You know you're a target
Of systematic schemes
Aimed to destroy you
By all means

Be wise and score
Don't fall for the traps
Jail's revolving door
Graveyards and mishaps

From sly enticements
Turn immediately away
Shed no innocent blood
Or you'll have to pay

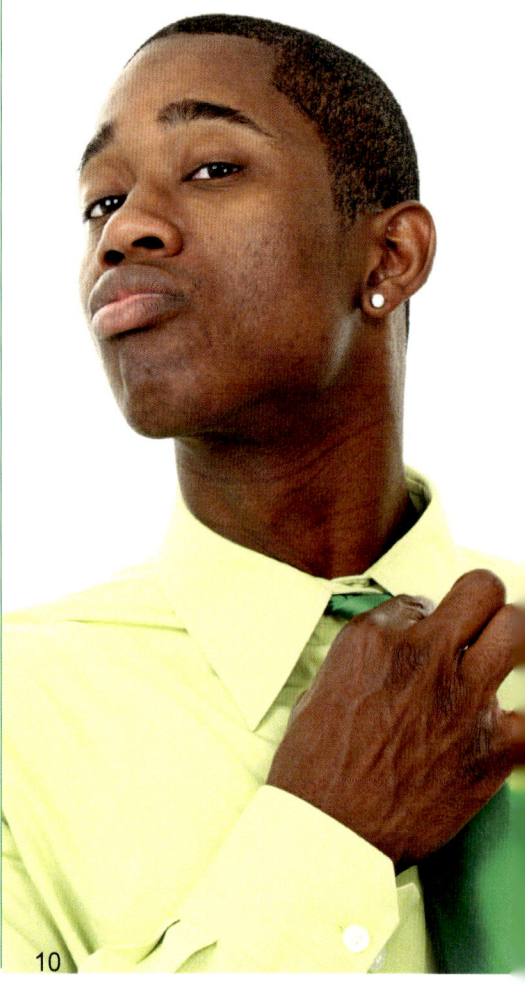

Guns are instruments
For death and despair
Family loss and grief
Just too much to bear

Beware of crime
In the making
Plans to steal
And lives taking

Another serious area
Of precaution and warning
Is sexual relations
AIDs and STDs alarming

Women and girls
May pursue after you
Best control yourself
Child support will come due

Education and knowledge
Are a good place to start

Stay in school
From the unlearned depart

All things considered
You can be weak or strong
The choice is yours
To do right or wrong

Need help to do right
You can always pray
Creator is close by
Never far away

Husband, father, brother,
Uncle, nephew, cousin, friend
Please preserve your life
So we all can win

See you're quite powerful
Because what you do
Affect so many
Not just a few

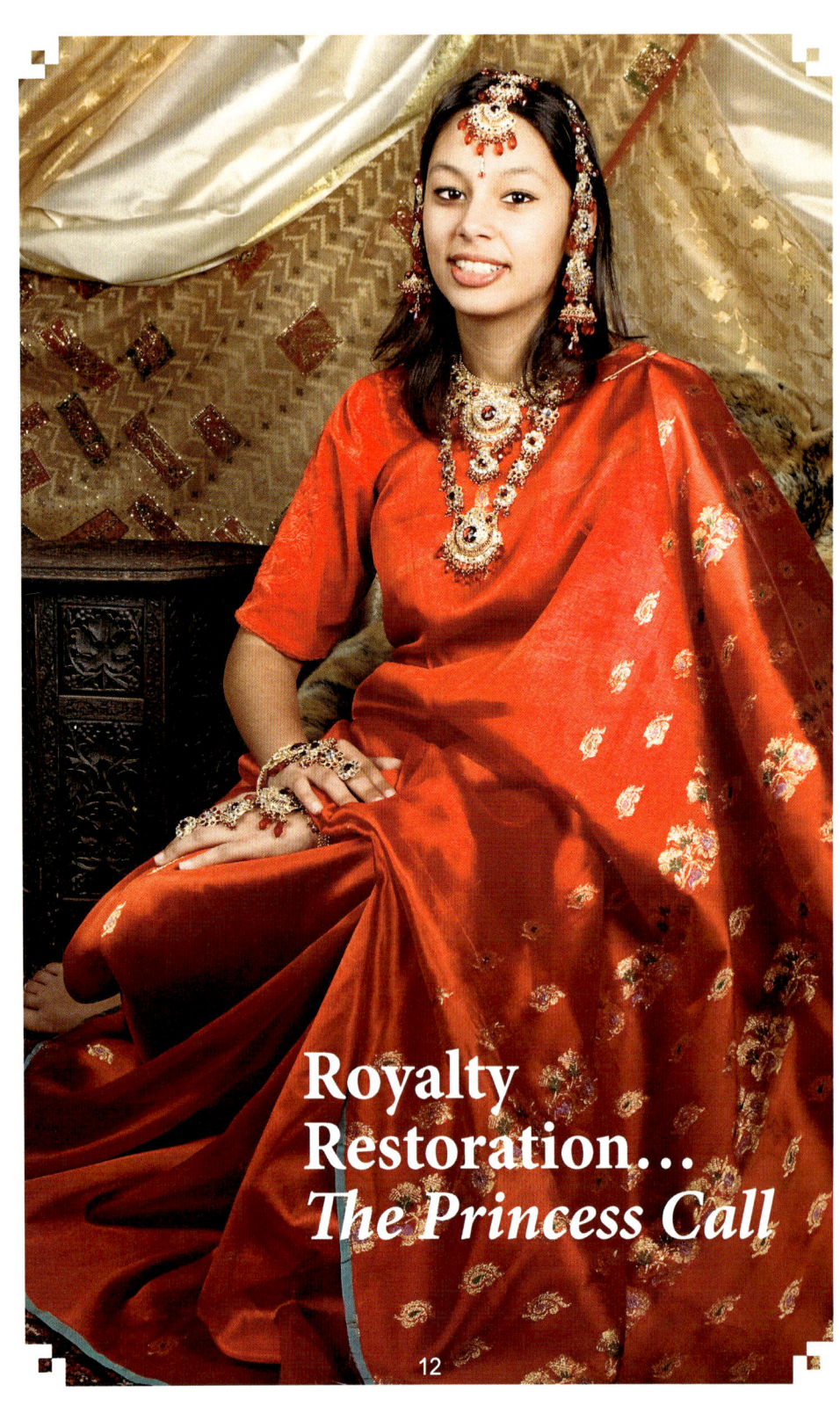

Calling all princesses
Your Father and King
Is looking for you
To restore your reign
In a world that exploits
And causes you pain
So your royal status
You can reclaim

Where they've exposed you
The King wants to robe you
With regal attire
That you will admire
Accenting beauty just fine
Without exposing the behind

It's a higher code of fashion
For damsels to be blessed
A call to do something
For sisters under dressed

Rebel against dirty music
And sex pot videos
Sisters can be gorgeous
Without looking like whores

They've labeled you dumb
But they were so wrong
Here's some action advice
A new beat with a new song!

Start your boycott
Start it now
Record companies will bow
To your wish
And your command

As you unite
And make a stand
Money honey
They understand

Say, "No more mean
and nasty songs"
Disrespect
It is wrong

Young ladies arise
Take it no more
Reject their lies
You're no whore!

Reject their skimpy, wimpy clothes
Replace them with royal pose
Design your own
Clothes and things
Set your own
Fads and trends

Will you dare
To think this far
Open your mind
You're smarter
You're a star

This will surely blow their minds
Let your royal gowns flow
Let your trade winds blow
Creativity…more, more, more!

Rich designers
you will scare
If you will
If you dare

Respecfully Yours

You can have me
Let me be yours
Share me with others
On your life tours

Whether at home
Out about or at school
I'll help you to master
The Golden Rule

Doing unto others
As you'd have them treat you
Is a realistic goal
I will help you to do

When I'm in your mind
And I'm in your heart
I'll come out in your words
All cursing will depart

With me, poor attitudes
And personality flaws
Can be swapped for gratitude
And a more noble cause

Parents, Teachers and Elders
Relatives and Peers
Will know you have something
They like with no fears

Usher has fortune
Justin Bieber has fame
But without respect
They'll lose their good names

Yes, I am Respect
To you may I belong?
To treat yourself and others
The right way, not wrong

Dog B-Gone-It!

Don't accept it
Because it's a lie
A word so wicked
It has made many cry

Obliviously spoken
Lost boys use it
To address girls
Who don't refuse it

The epitome
Of low-life words
It tears down
Each time it's heard

"B" this
And "B" that
Mouth so poison
Could D-Con a rat

Your mind and soul
You must clean
Become whole
Build self-esteem

You don't have to take
Being called a dirty name
Refuse the word "bitch"
Because it's profane

Webster defines it
As a dog-like animal
You are a young lady
Not a four-legged mammal

Enough is enough!
"Dog b-gone-it!"

Be Real

The world is out there
To be dealt with
    We know
But don't let it corrupt you
The process is dangerous
    Say no!

Be yourself
No matter what
    You're you

It pays to be real
Authentic appeal
The "true you" fulfill
    Be real

Money plays its part
In everyday living
    We know
But to get cash
Please don't sell
    Your soul

Secure the better things
That can't be bought
    Or sold
There's joy and peace of mind
Which come from within
And don't ever forget
A true and loyal friend

This knowledge
You should know
You reap what you sow

It pays to be real
With genuine stamp and seal
Nothing phony in the deal
Cease the drama
And just chill
    Be real

It pays to be real

Come Clean

Come clean
Come clean

No need of acting mean
    To your daddy
    Or your momma
    To your teachers
    Stop the drama

Come clean
Come clean

Disconnect from evil schemes
    Lying, stealing
    Drugs dealing
    Blood spilling
    Stop the killing

The gang can't
Always be there
Like God Almighty
Who is everywhere

So listen up
So you won't go down
You have life now
 So stick around

Come clean
Come clean

Wash more than your jeans
    More than your body
    And your hair
    Release all dirt
    From your care

Wash your mouth
Of filthy words
Dirty language
Shouldn't be heard

Come clean
Come clean

While you're livin'
It's not too late
Jesus Christ
Can set you straight
Receive forgiveness
And change your fate

Come clean
Come clean

Deal with your self-esteem
    God formed you right
    In his perfect sight
    And his image
    You are like

Jeans Too Tight With Me

Jeans closer than any friend
Sticks with me
Through thick and thin
Walks with me
Everywhere I go
Whether I'm running
Or moving slow

Close with me
On the scene
Time together lengthy
Forever it seems
Won't separate
But always clings

My ace boon coon
Whether early or late
Morning, night and noon
No matter what date
We dance to the tune
At a rhythmic rate

Perhaps with me
Jeans just too tight
To be this close
Don't seem quite right
On my space to impose
Such intimate might

So maybe after all
We're not a good fit
Have to stand tall
Cause I can hardly sit
Best for the mall
Where walking is a hit

Jeans very tight too
With ladies, girls and teens
But strange men may pursue
When aroused by your jeans
Danger can easily brew
If jeans too snug on you

Jeans are more loyal
To Levi than to us
And not that royal
If worn to stir lust
See jeans sold out
So big profits plus

Jeans so popular
Seen all around
Both near and far
To casually abound
Unknown or a star
On them denim's found

By now it's evident
Jeans no person
But pants prevalent
A fashion excursion
Today so relevant
What stylish coercion

Yeah, jeans too tight with
me… and you, too

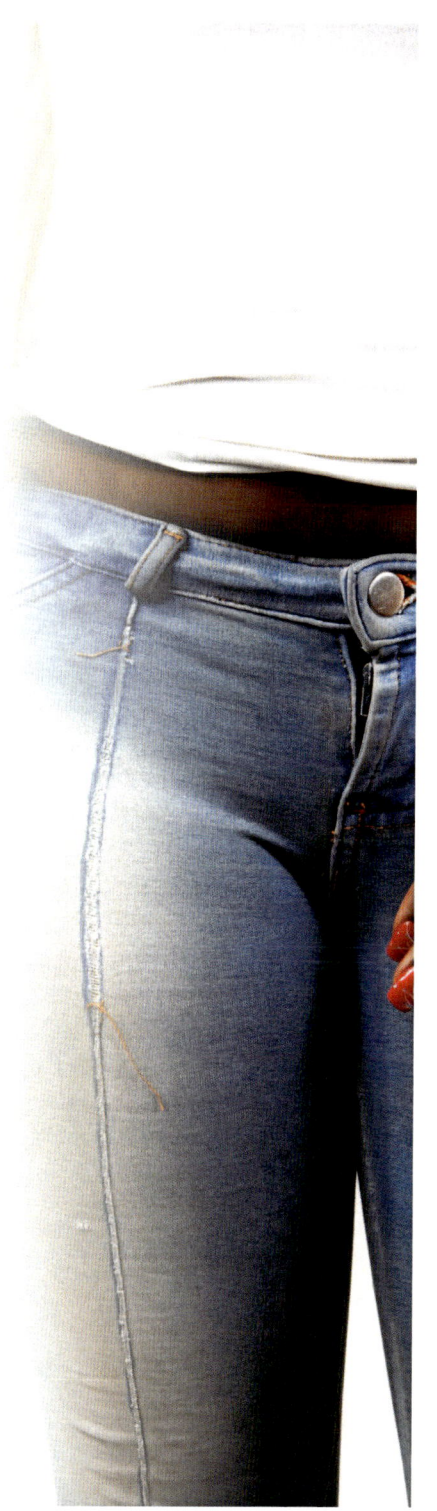

Meet Me @ the Mall

Weekend is here
Gonna have a ball
On my way with cheer
Meet me @ the mall

No need to be bored
Like a flower on the wall
Team's played and scored
Meet me @ the mall

Have very little money
Can't buy much at all
But I can walk and look honey
Just meet me @ the mall

Voice of wisdom says:

Hanging out at the mall
Can be lots of fun
But too unproductive
When the day is done

Instead of just looking
Wishing for money to pay
Think of business ideas
From merchandise on display

Don't be a consumer puppet
Pulled by corporate purse strings
That entice foolish spending
But won't give back a thing

Next time you go "malling"
With buddies casually free
Enjoy but be aware
There's more to it than you see

Response to wisdom:

Weekend plans underway
Now when I call
More insightfully I'll say
Meet me @ the mall

Cell Phone Chat...Possibilities

I've got to connect
Call my girlfriend back
Every minute I can
I'm talking to a friend

We talk about this
We text about that
Everything from who's fine
To baby phat

Minutes fly by
I've used them up
This chatting jones
Is costing big bucks

For all the talk
I net little return
Yet, I stay on my cell
Even though my ears burn

See my generation
We talk @ all costs
The cell phone companies
Are never at a loss

With conversation obsession
A lot's on the line
Family, grades, dreams, career
And yes, my time

Instead of us
And our parents paying the tab
Let's consider ways to profit
From our gift to gab

Consider other contests
With various categories
Including photos and texts
That tell the best stories

A consumer cell phone
Communication museum
Would preserve artistic messages
In the technical realm

Then looking forward
And reflecting back
We'd see it all began
With a cell phone chat

Just a Text Send

there are many words
that I send
to keep in touch
with my friends

just a text send

message clear
no voice needed
grab that phone
and simply read it

just a text send

me and my buddies
stay connected
no time to talk
we just text it

letter by letter
word by word
form the best messages
never heard

just a text send

P.S.
a life-saving rule
we must not bend
while driving
no text send

Rejecting 'Sexting'

Texting, texting
Day and night
Kinda boring to some
So they left what's right

Provocative photos
Observed a lot
Can eventually evolve
Into an elicit plot

Sent pictures and words
Shameful to see
Are in phone company files
For authorities

Breaking the law
Plus embarrassment
Can ruin reputations
Of sexting participants

So when texting
Turns to sexting
Protect yourself
By simply rejecting

Socialite Craze in Cyberspace

I claimed my space
My own address
My page and place
Where I recess

Invited my friends
So many connected
Emails piling in
Accepted and rejected

Posted photos and messages
And so did they
Checked all the time
Throughout the day

My Space was exciting
For quite a while
But Facebook came
With a better style

My brother's on Twitter
My sister's LinkedIn
Even the babysitter
Is a fb friend

It's about that time
Got the log-on urge
I must go online
Get my energy surge

My laptop and cell
Is right on hand
All is working well
With my internet plan

How I keep pace
Is an amazing grace
For my socialite craze
In cyberspace

Want nice things
By all means
They look so good
Buy 'em if I could

One boring day
I found a way
Received a credit card
With a limit large

Shopping I went
With one intent
Get things I desire
With a swipe by wire

Bill came in
Saw it and screamed
Didn't have a dime
To pay it on time

A month passed by
That peace wouldn't last
Phone rings night and day
Creditors bugging me to pay

Couldn't charge nothing else
And had no money left
Deep in financial trouble
Interest made the balance double

Stay clear of the credit card mess
So you don't flunk the credit test
Just in case you don't know
Learn about your FICO score

The Fair Isaac Credit Organization
Compiles and manages financial information
Fair and Isaac, two smart men
Established a system for creditors to lend

Experian, TransUnion and Equifax
Gather and report your financial stats
So find what's in their files on you
To determine if they're false or true

Warning you before you're fooled
About credit you must be schooled
Check your credit free once a year
At AnnualCreditReport.com, hear

Please, please listen up
Foolish spending stop abrupt
Can't afford a financial nap
You must avoid the credit trap

CONSPIRACY Revealed

There's a plot
There's a scheme
Against you children
And you teens

It's insane
It's obscene
Designed by satan
and it's mean

I did spy
I did hear
Their filthy plans
In my ear
Shhh, shhh
Listen dear

They said:
Use the record companies
Use their music
To defile the seed
Stir up violence
Sex and greed

Get their minds
At all costs
I want to be
Their only boss

Kill their boys
Kill them now
The seed they carry
Destroy it somehow!

For the ones
On church pews
I've got some
Baaad news

Turn their hearts
From their God
Make them dumb
Who were smart

Nasty music
And videos
Defile their girls
So they look like "hoes"

Scary, scary
Quite contrary
Virgins no more
Never to marry

Babies, babies
Make them cry
Daddies keep
In disguise!

Crack their minds
Crack their hearts
Crack, crack, crack
Will be their gods

Ha ha ha
Hee hee hee
We can destroy
Their families!

I heard them laugh
It made me mad!
I looked around
Yeah, we'd been had!!

I cried
I prayed
On the altar
I laid

God what can we do?
We've lost so many
The laborers are few

He said, *Go*
Hold back no more
Expose their schemes
Kick' em out the door

Tell them now!
Who their enemy is
Satan and his demons
Whispers in their ears

*Lies, lies, lies, lies
Told to youth
For their demise
Know the truth
And you'll be wise*

*They scheme to turn
Brother against brother
So with burning anger
They kill one another*

*Up, up, up
Wake them up
Shake, shake, shake
Shake them up
Let them know
I'll fill their cup*

God's chosen you children
And selected you teens
To expose the enemy
And his wicked schemes

Jesus said come to Him
Just as you are
He won't condemn
He's close, not far

From the streets
And broken homes
Come to Him
You're not alone

Come clean with God
He'll forgive your sins
From every bad thing
You can be cleansed

So rise mighty army
You're tough I know
We'll turn you to
Righteous soldiers pro

What you've gone through
And what you've seen
Prepared you for
This battle team

Snatch your thoughts
Take them back
From the gutter
Leave no slack

Reading the scriptures
Will help your mind
Bible's on the net
Do a search and find

So pray to God
From your heart
He's given you power
For a fresh start

Consider	Just like	On and off	Education	Don't unplug
Your future	A storm	Switches	Gives light	Your power
Without it	Power outage	Won't work	To do best	For success

Stay in school

Be Not 'Drugged' Along

There are forces at work
To get you to go
Where you don't need to be
To get you to view
What you don't need to see
To get you to stop
Being drug free

Hope you're aware
But haven't tried
Any type of drugs
To get you high
It's a dead end street
To make you deny
A problem so bleak
'Til users cry

Stimulants, depressants,
hallucinogens, narcotics
and every illegal drug
Damage spirit, mind and body
Hook and wire you
Then pull the plug

Learn what to avoid
If you don't know
The slew of drugs
"Pot", pills, "rocks" and "snow"
It's a hard, cold life
NOT the way to go

Be Not Drugged Along

What-ever!

Stuff keeps happening
Crazy it seems
Don't know why
The world is so mean
    What-ever!

Shootings occurring
Day after day
The death of peers
Won't go away

Determined to handle it
Not losing my cool
For all the commotion
There's a verbal coping tool
    What-ever!

Can't help but wonder
If this word works
Just gotta say something
When craziness lurks
    What-ever!

Home and school
Can be a trip
No one knows
How my mind could slip
    What-ever!

My generation
Uses this word to cope
In a trying situation
We say it and mope
    What-ever!

We see and hear
Any and everything
But we go on to school
And try to remain
        What-ever!

Schools and colleges
Are now danger zones
Angry souls vent bullets
From guns they own

So we press on with courage
Though fear lingers close
Because education counts
And offers the most
        What-ever!

No other appropriate word
In our language was found
To describe all the stuff
From which we rebound
        What-ever!

"What-ever" describes
 What we're dealing with
We speak while in motion
Moving on and being swift

If our grandparents had faced
This multiple evil intent
They'd probably respond
With a word equivalent
        To what-ever!

Come on help us out
Don't label us "X"
Declare us bad
And turn your backs
        But what-ever!

"Whatever" speaks loud
And it speaks clear
So young we handle it
Scared to even fear
        What-ever!

This important word
Spoken by youth much
Helps us transcend chaos
So understand and stay in touch

But if not, what-ever!

It's up to you
To make that move
To prepare and improve
To use the proper tools
So that you never lose
Your dream

It's your choice
To conquer fear
Or hold doubt near
To apply your faith
Don't hesitate
So that your dream
Can be seen

Embrace your growth
As your character is built
Your dream will not wilt
Establish it with integrity
To extend its longevity
Living now futuristically

On God's sure foundation
Stand in command
With your heart's desire
And the Master's plan
Steadily moving
Toward your promised land

You have the power
To stay the course
Drawing from divine source
As you continuously create
So building your dream
Can begin this date

Now pursue your dream
Like never before
You'll spot opportunity
Like an open door

And as you move
From your comfort zone
You'll find the strength
To carry on

Merge with your dream
United you're a winning team
No longer is it just inside
It's in your talk, your walk
Your stride

And when your dream
Becomes one with you
Then you'll know
It has come true

Saint Teen! Saint Teen!
God's calling you!
He knows you're ready
For something new

Roll up your sleeves
Roll out your heart
Receive right now
What I impart

Rise up and march
Your Savior's large
Make sure His Spirit
Is in your heart

You'll cast out demons
And they will flee
You'll speak with power
To the en-e-my
And scatter evil
 Princi-pal-i-ties

This army you're in
Is more than you know
Angels from heaven
Are backing your flow
And what's even more?
You're the ones to score!

SAINT TEEN

PEW PRESSURE

I know you can't stand it
    Religion
Deep down you made a
    Decision
To get out without a
    Collision
Or even causing
    Division

Because you're sick of the pew!

Pewie, pewie, pewie, pew
Church please get a clue
We ain't the breed
That you once knew
We're end-time warriors
For action new

What is this we're made to do?
It's not productive
For God or you
Rituals, traditions
Ceremonies, prisons

We're breakin' out
We're breakin' out
We can't afford
To close our mouths
There's got to be
A better route
This ain't real
It never heals
Sitting on the pew
While the enemy kills

Pewie, pewie, pewie, pew
Sitting longing
Wish we knew
The reason for sitting
So long on the pew

Pewie, pewie, pewie, pew
To cope with this
Ongoing dilemma
We sit in the back
To just chill and simmer

Pewie, pewie, pewie, pew
Sitting so much
Has spoiled you
Sunday after Sunday
Year after year
Ever learning
But never clear

We've got more
We've got to go
Our generation
Can't be that slow

Last days upon us
Time running out
About God's business
We must be devout

Pewie, pewie, pewie, pew
Out with the old
In with the new!

"Behold, I will do a new thing.
Now it shall spring forth;
shall you not know it?
*   - Isaiah 43:19*

No Bullying!

Bullying hurls intimidation
Intelligence it conceals
Peace it interrupts
While evil it reveals

Hateful, destructive
Disrespectful, disruptive
Mean, ugly and bad
Bullying is sad

Name-calling, cursing
And other word attacks
Pushing, shoving, hitting
Can't be handled with lax

If you see or experience bullying
In school or any placc
Tell parents, teachers or police
So the problem is faced

Those who bully
Are confused inside
Terrifying others
So their own flaws hide

Don't follow along
With a bully's scheme
You know it's wrong
Keep your ways clean

Bullying is more serious
Than it ever appears
Many have died
Overwhelmed by peer fear

Let's join together
To stop bullying insults
In person and online
We must improve results

Opt Out of Violence

The low road of violence
Is traveled without delay
Explosive, deadly anger
Leads to killings each day

Wiser ways exist
For resolving conflict
So if you're at risk
Read on, persist

If you're fighting mad
With urge to injure or kill
Take time to cool off
Pray, go away and chill

Then seriously contemplate
All whom you will hurt
Beyond that foe you hate
Both families' tragic alert

For such a vicious act
In jail or grave you'll land
Why mess up your life?
It's just a losing plan

Get control of yourself
You are more than how you feel
God put power inside of you
To clean up emotional spill

Release anger now
Break its hold on you
Be no more its slave
Your mind and ways renew

Temptation to hit or shoot
You know what it's about
Apply what you've learned
To violence, opt out

The Power Choice

Sacred is virginity
No matter what you've heard
It's linked to your identity
To be protected and preserved

Sex outside of marriage
Stirs confusion in heart and head
As a horse behind a carriage
Out of order and nowhere led

The world uses sex
Dangling it like bait
To lure and temp one
Into an impure state

Certainly you are free
To explore this danger zone
But be warned if you enter
You're most likely on your own

Sweet words sound good
Sensual touches can sway
But sharing your body
Don't make lovers stay

If you are being pressured
To have sex with someone
Get away from them quickly
It's a game called con

When pregnancy results
From a short affair
Plans for baby are slighted
Parents' relations can't bear

Many have felt exempt
From contracting a disease
But later went numb
When diagnosed with STDs

Few know the real deal
About sexual involvement
Demons of former lovers
Invade without consent

Intimacy with your partner
May seem fine at first
But trouble soon comes in
Soul ties makes it worst

Deluded and infatuated
Soul ties make you weak
Accepting a bad relationship
Seeming helpless to keep

Preserve personal power
Let no one defuse your might
Save yourself for matrimony
Gain pure living insight

The Deceptive Duo

Don't be deceived
By the Deceptive Duo
Many they've grieved
With tactics so low

Sometimes they come boldly
Other times in disguise
No matter how they come
It's to someone's demise

Sex and Violence
Are aggressively infiltrating
To dismantle innocence
From babies to teens dating

Systematically infusing
Young minds with smut
To hold them hostage
In the grip of lust

Creeping and crawling
Through the air
From television comes
Their hypnotic stare

Slowly brainwashing
The subconscious mind
With day after day
Of bloody crime

Through the shots
The blood and tears
Sex and violence
Enter eyes and ears

When it seems
No damage is done
Their criminal victims
Suddenly kill someone

City after city
Lives they claim
Yet somehow
They escape blame

Sex and violence fool
Whomever they can
In ways many people
Don't understand

Games, music, movies
TV and internet
Are channels they use
To stir lust and fret

Slimy, subtle and venomous
As a poisonous snake
Sex and violence destroy
At an alarming rate

Sexually transmitted diseases
They totally disregard
Like HIV and AIDS
Infecting deathly charge

The entertainment industry
Embraces the deadly pair
Like Sodom and Gomorrah
Corruption is all but rare

But who will dare
To tell the truth
Be politically incorrect
Persecuted and aloof

This spirit of whoredom
Runs wild on the loose
Manipulating the weak
To rape, murder and abuse

Committing child porn
Without relent
Heartless scavengers
Who don't repent

Be vigilant and alert
As a watchman on the wall
Keep children close by
To hear their cry and call

Learn to detect
In person and on the net
The sly, slick and wicked
Their offers, please reject

Look at You... You're Beautiful!

If beauty is truly in the beholder's eyes
Then I stand before you unable to disguise
The aesthetic magnetism that draws my very essence
As I gaze in the illumination of your powerful presence

Whether you know or not
God made you purposefully
Like stars in the sky
You shine brilliantly

Fellow brothers and sisters
Your faces are divinely shaped
All forms, shades and sizes
So richly innate

Thought I had somewhat figured you out
It's just now that I know what you're about
Look at you ... you're beautiful!

I bet you thought that I was through
There's so much more to admire about you
Look at you ... you're beautiful!

Your spirituality, individuality
And survival techniques
Are enough to knock an elephant
Upside down off his feet

With awe I admire you
You're dressed so nice
In your love and your strengths
For your garments can't be measured
They surpass the greatest lengths
Look at you ... you're beautiful!

Then there's your coldness, anger, envy
Misunderstandings, pains and hurts!
But it's in forgiving and making up
That your beauty really works
Look at you ... you're beautiful!

Seasons' Greetings

Spring

Arising from the earth,
arrayed in green,
my grass and leaves burst forth
blossoming in every color.
In a floral parade across the land,
I march in time to meet you annually,
Embracing you with warmth, vigor
and as a breath of fresh air.
I shower you with raindrops of blessings,
singing a rainbow melody
in vivid hues—I am Spring!

Freshly lingering with life;
Massaging aesthetic beauty
into the landscape of hills, valleys,
yards, minds and hearts;
Exciting the birds, bees, flowers and trees.
Therapeutically, through each
month of my stay,
a cycle of life is renewed.
Yes, I am Spring!

Summer

With the closeness of the sun,
I usher in the hotness of June, July and August.
With heated passion for life,
I make living considerably easier.
Generously, I extend daylight into the night,
relieving laborers and students
with vacations long overdue.

Why not melt in my embrace?
The heat is on
and won't linger long.
So enjoy me to the fullest.
Because soon,
I, Summer,
will be gone.

Fall

Fanning cool breezes
into the atmosphere ...
Slowly with majestic diplomacy,
Miraculously before all eyes,
I orchestrate with smooth splendor
a chlorophyll takeover in nature.

So beautifully executed,
my replacement of greenery
with hues of yellows, oranges, reds and browns
stimulate eyes and hearts
to accept the gradual change;
knowing that the slow takeover
will eventually lead
to every leaf's fall
and every green lawn's browning.
I am Fall!

Winter

Walking through the valley
of the shadow of death ... hiding life.
Covering it under the wings and strong winds
of my mighty Hawk.
Through layers of snow and icicles,
I appear as a grim reaper.
Harsh and bitterly cold,
I chill the warm-blooded with shivers
while they run to escape my dismal grip.
Yet, I render the unique beauty of snow
to cover the earth
with shimmering pure white flakes.
Then with my chilling hand of power
I withdraw the evidence of life in the plant kingdom,
leaving one exception to assure you
that life is well—the Evergreen.
But know that I've only held life
in mandatory hibernation
so that it's vivid expression
may be released once again to you.

Still, few really like me
and I'm labeled a bringer of death.
But please consider,
the death I bring,
makes way for resurrection.
I am Winter!

4 Seasons

We, the four seasons,
Spring, Summer, Fall and Winter,
work together.
Like us, you must move promptly
regarding your callings and personal seasons,
in respect of one another.
While you appear to overlap on occasions,
when it's your turn to come forth,
never turn away, wait, or withdraw.
Appreciate each one's uniqueness,
though never at the expense
of your own distinct splendor.
Allow one another time and space.
 Express all gifts completely.

As we seasons greet you with changes
so necessary to spice life
and deliver it from false perceptions
of blandness and boredom,
may you salute one another
through all the cycles of life
with the love, joy, peace,
passion and diversity
of Seasons' Greetings!

The kite dances over the ocean
It dips smoothly with the breeze
Twisting and turning wonderfully
With such rhythmic ease

Dipping and swerving above the tides
Sliding and gliding in the sky
Freely and softly on air it rides
With rapport to wind's reply

Let's dance in life like the kite
Airborne to lean and sway
With grace and warm delight
Not pushing or forcing our way

Freely ascend like the kite
Above chaos and unrest
Like a feather so very light
Never heavy with pressure or stress

Soar like the kite
Flying high without wings
Moving gracefully in flight
As its melodious motion sings

Dancing Over the Ocean…Kite Flight

Watch, Listen or Eject

Over and Over
And over again
Music, songs, videos, games
Heard, viewed, played
Heard, viewed, played
Heard, viewed, played
Over and over
And over again

Messages enter
Ears and eyes
Lyrics and visuals
Harmful or wise
Over and over
And over again

Consider
What you see
And listen to
Does it help prepare
You for success
or just tell you
to undress?
Does it suggest
You peacefully live
Or show you
Ways to kill?

Consider
The rappers
Celebrities you like
Are their personal lives
Rapped that tight?
Is what they say
Actually right?

Consider
Then select
Watch, listen
or eject

Good Thoughts Pursue

From nowhere it seems
A thought so terrible
Came on the scene
Immediately I thought
Did I think that?
Knowing its fault
I had to reject

Any kind of thought
Can come at any time
But if it's negative
Just simply decline

Destructive thinking
Is so much like
An alcoholic drinking
The first sip
The biggest mistake
The next nip
Your soul it takes

Imagine, if you will
The trouble we'd avoid
Replacing thoughts that kill
With ones of good accord

We have dominion
To rule over our thoughts
Not based on opinion
But principles and laws

Discard dirty thoughts
That smell like manure
And think positive ones
Constructive and pure

As you think in your heart
So are you
Therefore be smart
Good thoughts pursue

"… Whatever things are true, whatever things are noble, whatever things are just, whatever things are pure, whatever things are lovely, whatever things are of a good report; if there be any virtue and if there is anything praiseworthy—meditate on these things."   Philippians 4:8

trans-parent

We had just finished talking
about our parents — me and my friends.
Conversation was hot! ... and cold,
bitter and sweet, hateful and loving,
painful and pleasant, disrespectful
and honorable, void and full.

As gifted and intelligent as we all were,
each of our parents had some
serious issues; at least according to our
perceptions and descriptions. Felt like I'd
been on a seesaw, merry-go-round,
or something!
You know what I'm saying?

Now, alone again, I thought I'd
catch some Zzz's.
Instead, I entered into another zone.
My head was spinning.
I held it but it didn't stop
what happened next.

I opened my eyes in Where!!!?
"Parentland!"
I wanted so bad for it to be Paradise
but it was what it was—"Parentland."
Another sign said "Rated PG."
I thought, "Oh, I'm going to a movie."
It was a movie alright.
Before me, each scene flashed vividly.
I saw my friends and their parents.
I had a birdseye view, like a fly on the wall.

There was Amelia's mom.
She was hugging Amelia with reassurance
when in came a strange man.
He checked out Amelia like
she was a grown woman.
Her mom accepted money from him and
left her alone in the room with him.

He began to touch her in the wrong way
as she struggled to get away from him.
But the man overpowered her and began to
rape her. Outraged, I was ready to jump on
him in my friend's defense but couldn't do a
thing. I was invisible to them and unable to
do anything about what I saw.
I thought, "This is a nightmare."

All of sudden I was viewing another scene.
It was Jawaun's dad and he was high as a
kite, smoking a pipe and drinking liquor.
When Jawaun walked into the room, he
said, "Here, take a puff and a drink. You're
about to be a man now." Though reluctant,
his dad convinced him to indulge. I never
knew until then, why Jawaun had a
drug problem.

Quickly, I moved to another scene. There,
was Kaylon's dad, mom, brother and sister.
They all looked so frightened, except his
dad. He began to curse at them all. He was
furious for no apparent reason.
Then he slapped their mom and shoved
her to the floor. She was crying and
screaming. Kaylon went to jump on his dad
but his dad pulled out a gun and yelled,
"Don't you dare or I'll kill all of you.

The room was silent as they all froze. Then their dad, looking at their mom, said, "Forgive me honey. I just got a little angry. You know I love you all to death."
Scared to disagree, they all begin to act like it had never happened.
Off I went to the next scene.

I cried out "STOP, I can't take anymore." But there I was at the next scene.
To my surprise, it was much more pleasant than prior scenes. I saw Breanna's parents. They showed her lots of love but lived in different homes. They had divorced seven years ago when Breanna was 8. I saw Breanna going back and forth from one house to the next. Her father was remarried and her stepmom merely tolerated her the weekends she spent with her dad. I could tell Breanna was not happy but she wanted her parents to be. On I went to the next scene.

This time it was my parents. I had caused a few problems to say the least. I saw them visiting my school to talk with my teachers; making me be respectful, do my chores my homework and to go to bed at a certain time. For all this discipline, I couldn't stand my parents. I stormed to my room on many occasions without my cell phone. Plus the internet and TV were off limits until I improved my attitude. While many of my buddies texted, talked and surfed the web through the night, I was bored to sleep. Just as I began to think, "What stale parents I have," I had flashbacks of previous scenes.

Then I had a vision into the future of how my friends' lives were adversely affected by their parents. The abuse and divorce had hurt them so deeply, that the pain and emotional damage they suffered may take many years to overcome. This made me realize how blessed I was to have the kind of parents I had. I realized I could have been in one of the other scenes. Also, I understood that even if I had, I still would need to forgive my parents, so I could move on with my own life.

No matter how good or awful parents may be, we, their children, have the power to forgive, respect and love them anyway. Never let this power be stripped from you. If it has been, get it back, one day at a time. Give your mom and/or dad a card to show you care. Pray and get help if you need to. But by all means, see beyond the surface of your parental situation.

See "trans-parent."

FORGIVENESS BEGIN

Life's not always fair
Or right
Situations happen
In spite
Of family ties
Friendly connections
Committed relations
Good intentions
Dedication and loyalty
Gifts and abilities
Trust or innocence

Offences or violations
Will come
Betrayal explodes
Like a bomb
Hurt and pain fall
Like rain
What was once pure
Is stained
The question is will you
Love again?
Will you forgive?
You can
One step at a time
Just begin

Don't try to figure out how
Why or when
Pray asking God
For a hand
Forgiveness is not a foe
But a friend
So pry your heart open
And begin

Youth Empowerment Affirmations
(YEA)

I am wonderfully made with awesome potential.

I am totally unique, so I will not compare myself with others.

I have God-given dominion on this earth to access resources and to use them wisely.

I have access to education and I vow to take full advantage by studying, being respectful to my parents, teachers, peers and others.

I put my mind into learning mode and I will read, participate and learn in all my classes, even if I don't like them.

Because my future is at stake, I go beyond what I want to do, to what I need to do.

I need to prepare for my future, so I'm making a commitment to read, study, do my homework and learn all I can.

I am smart and I have an excellent mind. I think clearly and make wise choices.

I refuse to listen to anyone who tries to sway me into making bad choices for my life.

I excel in all I do.

This is my life and I will make good choices that help me to be successful and in a position to give back to my family and my community.

I will pray, get counseling and work on the issues and problems that are hindering and hurting me.

I love myself, so I can learn to love God and others.

I do not have to take any more abuse of any kind from others because I will tell someone who can help me. Plus, I will get away from anyone who disrespects me verbally, physically or mentally.

I am an overcomer and I will succeed.

I will begin to write down my ideas.

I will pursue my dreams.

I will become a _____ and/or a _____.

I will search and find out what I need to do to prepare to be a _____.

I will go to and talk with at least two people who are already doing what I want to do.

I have the favor of God and people.

I attract people who will help me and I will do at least one good deed per day to help someone.

I am a winner!

Hotlines to Help Directory

There is help for real life problems and situations. You may be worried about a friend or have some issues of your own. Not getting help only allows more time for the problem to get worse. The organizations below provide confidential help to thousands of young people who are hurting, abused or just in trouble. The people at these organizations are there because they want to help. Hotlines are designed to help you handle any kind of crisis. They can offer support or guidance when you need it most.

Please remember, if you have a serious emergency, always call 911 or the police first.

Bullying

The National Center for Bullying Prevention: 1-888-248-0822; helps to promote awareness and teach effective ways to respond to bullying; www.Pacer.org/bullying.

STOMP Out Bullying: 1-855-790-HELP (4357); focused on reducing bullying and cyber bullying; www.StompOutBullying.org.

StopBullying.gov: provides information from various government agencies on how kids, teens, young adults, parents, educators and others in the community can prevent or stop bullying.

StopTheBullying.com: 1-407-617-3807 or 1-407-579-7001; provides Bullying Prevention Awareness for schools' staffs, teachers, administrators, and parents.

TeensAgainstBullying.org: created by and for teens as a place for middle and high school students to find ways to address bullying, to take action, to be heard, and to join an important social cause.

Victims of Crime Help Line: 1-800-FYI-CALL (1-800-394-2255), 1-800-211-7996 TTY. The National Center for Victims of Crime refers callers to an array of critical services, including crisis intervention, research information, and assistance with the criminal justice process, counseling and support groups. Visit www.NCVC.org.

Child Abuse

Childhelp USA, National Child Abuse Hotline: 1-800-4-A-CHILD® (1-800-422-4453); offer services for victims, offenders, and parents, providing prevention and treatment, and receives calls from throughout the U.S., Canada, the U.S. Virgin Islands, Puerto Rico, and Guam; www.ChildHelp.org.

Cyber Tipline: 1-800-843-5678; for reporting the exploitation of children, such as child pornography. Parents and others concerned with child safety can call this number to report suspicious or illegal Internet activity online; operated by National Center for Missing and Exploited Children.

National Center for Missing and Exploited Children (NCMEC): 1-800-THE-LOST or 1-800-843-5678. Report any information regarding a missing child. If you know about a child who is in immediate risk or danger, call local law enforcement.

Dating Abuse

DoSomething.org: Text HELPME to 38383 or Email helpme@dosomething.org; a proactive educational youth advocacy entity fighting sexual assault and dating abuse.

National Teen Dating Abuse 24-hour Helpline: 1-866-331-9474 and 1-866-331-8453 TTY; 4 p.m. - 2 a.m. CST; provides critical help and counseling to teens experiencing dating abuse. Visit www.LoveIsRespect.org.

Break The Cycle's Teen Helpline: 1-888-988-8336; an education and prevention organization to help youth with social and dating issues. Visit www.BreakTheCycle.com.

RAINN (Rape, Abuse and Incest National Network): 1-800-656-4673 or www.RAINN.org.

Domestic Violence

National Coalitions Against Domestic Violence (NCADV): 1-303-839-1852 and 1-303-839-8459 TTY; a grassroots non-profit membership organization, working since 1978 to end violence in the lives of women. Visit: www.NCADV.org. Email: mainoffice@ncadv.org.

National Domestic Violence/Child Abuse/Sexual Abuse: 1-800-799-7233.

National Sexual Assault Hotline: 1-800-656-HOPE (4673). The Rape, Abuse & Incest National Network (RAINN) operates this free and confidential hotline and is the nation's largest anti-sexual assault organization. Also, RAINN educates the public about sexual assault and leads national efforts to improve services to victims and ensure that rapists are brought to justice. Visit www.RAINN.org.

Drug & Alcohol Abuse

The Alcohol Hotline: 1-800-ALCOHOL (1-800-252-6465); a nationwide help and referral hotline for alcohol and drug problems. The phones are answered by individuals trained to assist callers 24 hours a day, seven days a week.

Alcoholics Anonymous: 1-212-870-3400; A.A. World Services, Inc.; a voluntary worldwide fellowship of men and women who meet together to maintain sobriety to live alcohol free. Visit www.AA.org.

Drug-Rehab.org: 1-888-206-2494; a non-profit drug and alcohol rehab referral and placement service with caring placement counselors.

Inspirations: 1-888-757-6237; a drug and alcohol rehab for teens helpline, providing extensive resources to help addicted teens and their families; www.InspirationsYouth.com.

Teen Challenge International, USA: 1-417-581-2181; provides youth, adults and families with an effective and comprehensive Christian faith-based solutions to life-controlling drug and alcohol problems in order to become productive members of society. Nearly 200 residential Teen

Challenge centers across the USA provide intensive help and care for people of all ages. Visit www.TeenChallengeUSA.com. Or email: info@teenchallengeusa.com.

Tobacco Free Quit Line: 1-877-724-1090.

Depression & Suicide

Boys Town National Hotline: 1-800-448-3000; 1-800-448-1833 TDD line; provides direct care to 31,000 children and families each year. Email: hotline@boystown.org; www.BoysTown.org.

National Hope Line Network: 1-800-442-HOPE, 1-800-442-4673 or 1-800-SUICIDE (1-800-784-2433); your connection to a certified, 24-hour crisis center.

National Suicide Prevention Lifeline: 1-800-273-TALK or 1-888-628-9454 for Spanish-speaking callers. This is the only federally funded hotline for suicide prevention and intervention.

Suicide Prevention Resource Center (SPRC): 1-877-438-7772; provides prevention support, training, and resources to assist organizations and individuals to develop suicide prevention programs, interventions and policies. Visit SPRC.org or email: info@sprc.org.

Youth America Hotline: 1-877-YOUTHLINE (1-877-968-8454); available to help teens in crisis, 3 p.m.-9 p.m. EST, CST, MST, and PST.

Gang Violence

Calgary Police Service, Canada: 1-403-206-8191; Teen Line 1-403-264-8336; committed to stopping the violence and preventing the criminal activity of gangs through its developed Organized Crime Operations Center (OCOC) resources; www.CalgarPolice.ca or www.GetALife.ca.

Crime Stoppers USA: 1-800-222-TIPS (8477) or 1-309-762-9500 (Always Anonymous); a citizen, media and police co-operative program designed to involve the public in the fight against crime; www.CrimeStoppersUSA.

Tariq Khamisa Foundation (TKF): 1-855-440-9607; dedicated to transforming violence prone, at-risk youth into nonviolent achieving individuals and create safe and productive schools; www.TKF.org.

We Tip Inc.: 1-800-78-CRIME (27463); a hotline to report information regarding gang violence and any major crime. Visit www.TippeCanoe.in.gov.

Health Issues

S.A.F.E. Alternatives: 1-800-DONTCUT® (1-800-366-8288); a nationally recognized treatment approach, professional network and educational resource base committed to helping youths and others achieve an end to self-injury behavior; www.SelfInjury.com.

ANAD - National Association of Anorexia Nervosa and Associated Disorders: 1-630-577-1330;M-F,12 p.m.-8 p.m. EST; dedicated to the prevention and alleviation of eating disorders; www.ANAD.org.

National Eating Disorders Association: 1-800-931-2237; providing help and hope to those affected by eating disorders; M-F, 11:30 a.m.-7:30 p.m. EST; www.EDPA.org.

National AIDS Hotline: 1-800-232-4636. This 24-hour hotline provides information, education, answers and questions regarding AIDS, testing facilities, and medications used for treatment.

National STD Hotline: 1-800-227-8922 and 1-800-344-7432 en Española; provides information on sexually transmitted diseases (STDs), such as chlamydia, gonorrhea, HPV/genital warts, herpes, and HIV/AIDS, and referrals to local clinics.

Poison Help: 1-800-222-1222. Call this number 24 hours a day, 7 days a week, to talk to a poison expert. Call right away if you have a poison emergency. Also, call if you have a question about a poison or about poison prevention.

Homelessness

The Covenant House: 1-800-999-9999; a confidential crisis hotline that operates 365 days a year, 4 p.m.-8 p.m. EST. Covenant House has houses in 21 cities throughout the United States, Canada, and Central America, providing love, caring, and vital resources needed to help a young person break away from life on the streets forever; www.NINELINE.org.

My Friend's Place: 1-800-339-6993 (an Emergency Food and Shelter line); a nonprofit Resource Center, offering a comprehensive continuum of care that includes free emergency resources such as food and clothing in combination with health, educational, and therapeutic services to over 1,600 homeless youth and their children each year. Visit www.MyFriendsPlace.com.

Human Trafficking

National Human Trafficking Resource Center (NHRTC): 1-888-373-7888. NHTRC is a program of the Polaris Project, a non-profit, non-governmental organization working exclusively on the issue of human trafficking, providing referrals, resources, general information, training and technical assistance. Visit www.PolarisProject.org.

The Chrysalis Network: 1-866-528-7109 Trafficking Support Line; offers a free, confidential trauma counseling service to women and men who have been trafficked and exploited for the purposes of commercial sex and forced labor; www.ChrysalisNetwork.org.

Pregnancy Health/Support

American Pregnancy Association: 1-800-672-2296; a national nonprofit for the promotion of pregnancy wellness and education; www.AmericanPregnancy.org.

America's Pregnancy Helpline: 1-866-942-6466 or 1-888-467-8466; www.AmericanPregnancy.org; American Pregnancy Association offers teens and young adults education and information about the things they want to know concerning pregnancy (anonymously and confidentially).

Feminists for Life of America: 1-703-836-3354; an advocacy organization to improve and increase practical resources, support and solutions that enable young pregnant women to choose life for their babies; www.FeministsForLife.org; also, www.KidsOnAShoestring.com.

Option Line: 1-800-395-4357; a national hotline offering a network of pregnancy centers throughout the U.S. and Canada that provide pregnancy tests and options counseling and support; www.OptionLine.org.

Stand Up Girl: www.StandUpGirl.com; provides encouragement, answer questions anonymously and do a live chats to help teen girls with problems and concerns.

Runaways

National Safe Place: Text SAFE to 69866. National Safe Place is launching a new project to help teens connect to a Safe Place location. The TXT 4 Help project uses technology to quickly offer teens information about the closest location where they can get immediate help and safety.

Here is how it works: Youth in crisis can text the word SAFE and their current location to the number 69866 and they will receive an address of the nearest Safe Place site and contact number for the local youth shelter. In cities that don't have a Safe Place program, the youth will receive the name and number of the youth shelter or, if there is no local shelter, a national-hotline number.

National Runway Switchboard: 1-800-RUNAWAY (1-800-786-2929), 1-800-621-4000 and 1-800-621-0394 TDD; a non- judgmental, confidential crisis intervention plus local and national referrals through a 24-hour hotline for youth and their families. Visit www.1800RUNAWAY.org.

General Help & Opportunities

Adolescent Crisis Team: 1-714-839-3388; dedicated in guiding parent/guardians through a struggling teen crisis; www.AdolescentCrisisTeam.com.

Focus Adolescent Services: 1-410-341-4216; M-F, 9 a.m.-5 p.m. EST; a clearinghouse that provides information and resources to empower individuals and entities to help teens and their families; www.FocusAS.com.

Teen Mania Ministries: 1-800-229-8336; offers many different opportunities for teens of all ages, including Acquire the Fire Events (atfinfo@teenmania.org); Extreme Summer Camps (campsinfo@teenmania.org); Global Expeditions (geinfo@teenmania.org); and Honor Academy (hainfo@teenmania.org); www.TeenMania.com.

Youth With A Mission (YWAM): 1-808-326-7228 or 1-808-326-4400. YWAM currently has over 16,049 full-time volunteer workers in nearly 1,100 operating locations in 171 nations and trains 25,000 short-term missions' volunteers annually.

Inspirational, Ministry, and Motivational Speaking

For over twenty-five years, Ms. Coleman has inspired diverse audiences through her innovative, national and regional radio and television programs, and her award-winning *Purpose* Magazine. As a deeply engaging speaker with a sparkling manner, she will motivate your audience through her wise and practical presentations. She speaks on a variety of topics, and recites her poetry at churches, schools, conventions, community affairs and corporate events.

TOPICS

Inspiration / Ministry:
The Power of Being Yourself
Come Out, Come Out, Where Ever You Are
20/20 Heart Vision: Beyond Appearances
The Process of You

Motivation:
Purpose in Process
Up To You
Double Dare To
Power Choices

Business:
Inter-Vision Dynamics   *Testing Grounds to Character*
Relationship Construction   *Balance Basics*
Practicing Priorities   *Strategies for Fulfillment*

Poetry for Younger and Older Generations

Ella Coleman has mentored and taught youth for more than two decades. As a business owner, she has worked with high schools, colleges and universities to provide internships, training and jobs for students. Because of her love for young people, she worked diligently to write and publish this book of poetry, *Youth Arise! A Poetic Call to Empowerment*.

Poetic Overflow is an inspirational book of poetry to inspire, edify, and challenge. It has been written to personify what really matters—God and His creation, especially people and their well-being. It is a word feast for readers to delightfully indulge.

For bookings and to order copies of *Youth Arise* or *Poetic Overflow* visit EllavationPublishing.com or email ellavatingu@live.com.